STAEHELIN MEYER

Diese Buchreihe versammelt die Bauwerke einzelner, mit hohem Qualitätsanspruch ausgewählter jüngerer Schweizer Architekten. Seit 2004 kuratiere ich die Reihe *Anthologie* in der Form einfacher Werkdokumentationen. Sie ist vergleichbar mit der «Blütenlese», wie sie in der Literatur für eine Sammlung ausgewählter Texte angewendet wird. Es liegt in der Natur des Architektenberufs, dass die Erstlingswerke junger Architekten meist kleinere übersichtliche Bauaufgaben sind. Sie sind eine Art Fingerübung, mit der sie das Erlernte anwenden und ihr architektonisches Sensorium erproben und entfalten können. Die Begabung und die Leidenschaft für das Metier lassen sich dabei früh in voller Deutlichkeit und Frische erkennen. So stecken in jedem der kleinen und grossen Projekte inspirierte Grundgedanken und Vorstellungen, die spielerisch und gleichermassen perfekt in architektonische Bilder, Formen und Räume umgesetzt werden. Damit wird mir wieder einmal bewusst, dass in der Architektur wie in anderen Kunstformen die Bilder und Ideen, die hinter dem Werk stehen, das Wesentliche sind. Es mag diese Intuition sein, die der Künstler hat, und die dann über sein Werk wie ein Funke auf den Betrachter überspringt, so wie es der italienische Philosoph Benedetto Croce in seinen Schriften eindringlich beschreibt.

Heinz Wirz
Verleger

This book series presents buildings by selected young Swiss architects that set themselves high quality standards. Since 2004, I have been curating the *Anthologie* series by simply documenting their oeuvre. The series can be compared to a literary anthology presenting a collection of selected texts. It is in the nature of the architectural profession that early works by young architects are mostly small, limited building tasks. They are a kind of five-finger exercise in which the architects apply what they have learnt, as well as testing and developing their architectural instincts. Talent and a passion for the profession can be seen at an early stage in all of its clarity and freshness. Each project, be it large or small, contains an inspired underlying concept and ideas that are playfully and consummately implemented as architectural images, forms and spaces. Thus, I am regularly reminded that in architecture, as in other art forms, the images and ideas behind the works are their essence. Perhaps this is the same intuition described so vividly by the Italian philosopher Benedetto Croce, one that is absorbed by the artist and flies like a spark via the work to the viewer.

Heinz Wirz
Publisher

STAEHELIN MEYER

QUART

UMBAU REIHENHAUS BIASCASTRASSE, BASEL
2010–2011

Das 1947 erstellte, mehrmals erweiterte kleinteilige Eckeinfamilienhaus wurde grundlegend modernisiert und durch grössere Eingriffe den Bedürfnissen der neuen Besitzer angepasst. Im Zentrum des Hauses positioniert sich als tragendes und gliederndes Element ein Betonkern mit integrierter Treppe, die das Wohngeschoss mit dem im Sockelgeschoss angeordneten Elternbereich verbindet. Aus den Seitenwänden der Treppe entwickeln sich einerseits die Küchenzeile und andererseits rückwärtig die Bibliothek, beide ebenfalls in Sichtbeton ausgeführt. Der neue Kern erlaubt, Wände abzubrechen und aus der kleinteiligen Struktur einen zusammenhängenden, mäandrierenden Wohnraum zu schaffen.

BIASCASTRASSE TERRACED HOUSE CONVERSION, BASEL
2010–2011

The closely partitioned single-family corner house, built in 1947 and extended several times, was thoroughly modernised and adapted to the needs of the new owners through extensive interventions. Connecting the living floor with the parents' area located in the basement, a concrete core with an integrated staircase is situated in the centre of the house as a load-bearing and organisational element. The staircase's lateral walls form a kitchen on one side and a library on the other, both likewise constructed in exposed concrete. The new core makes it possible to demolish walls and create a continuous, meandering living space out of the small-scale structure.

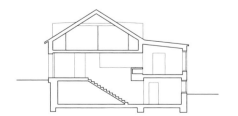

10 m

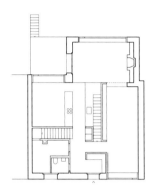

10 m

DOPPELEINFAMILIENHÄUSER RÜTIRING, RIEHEN
2011–2014

Zwei zueinander abgewinkelte, polygonale Baukörper erzeugen unterschiedlich ausgerichtete Wohnungen mit privatem Aussenbezug und spannen einen gemeinsamen parkartigen Aussenraum auf. Als Ersatz für die Attikafläche werden Wohn- und Atelierräume mit grosszügigen, im Hang liegenden Oberlichtern im Sockelgeschoss angeordnet. Das Herz der beiden Baukörper bildet jeweils ein tragender Kern, der Küche, Nasszellen und Ankleide beinhaltet. Die zentrale Anordnung aller dienenden Funktionen erlaubt entlang der Fassade zusammenhängende Wohn- und Schlafräume, die als Rundlauf begangen werden können. Massive Eiche, Beton, der aufs Korn geschliffene Unterlagsboden sowie der lasierte Gipsputz – alles rohe, beständige Materialien – prägen den Charakter der Innenräume.

RÜTIRING SEMI-DEATCHED HOUSES, RIEHEN
2011–2014

Two polygonal structures angled towards each other generate variously oriented apartments with private exterior connections and enclose a common park-like outdoor space between them. To replace the lost area, living and studio rooms with generous skylights positioned in the hillside were located in the basement. The heart of each structure is formed by a load-bearing core containing a kitchen, bathrooms and dressing rooms. The central arrangement of the service spaces creates connected living and sleeping rooms along the façade that can be accessed along a continuous loop. Solid oak, concrete, screed floors sanded to the granulate and stained gypsum plaster – all raw, durable materials – define the character of the interior.

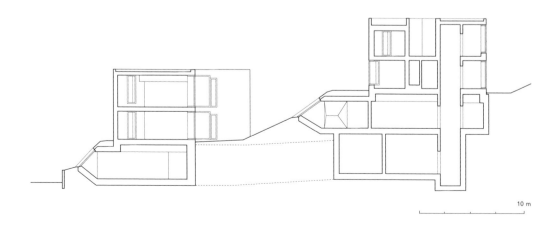

10 m

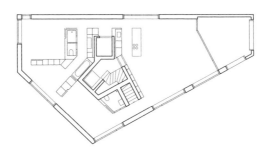

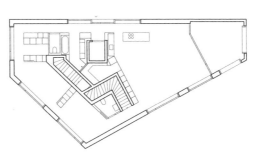

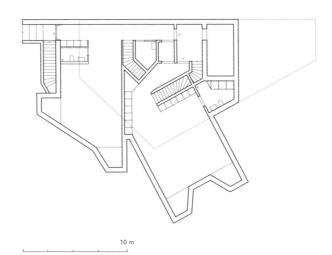

10 m

EINFAMILIENHAUS RESERVOIRSTRASSE, BASEL
2014–2016

Zwei tragende, als Schotten ausgebildete Wände definieren den in der Höhe gestaffelten, lang gezogenen Baukörper und fassen ihn seitlich. Das Erdgeschoss treppt sich, dem Terrainverlauf folgend, zum Garten hin ab. So entstehen in den verschiedenen Wohnzonen unterschiedliche Raumhöhen. Ein durch das Erd- und Untergeschoss geführter Innenhof gliedert und belichtet die Kernzone des Wohnbereichs sowie das Elternschlafzimmer mit Ankleide und Bad. Das Gegenüber des Innenhofs ist der Kern im Eingangsbereich, der die Nasszelle aufnimmt. Sämtliche Einbauten entwickeln sich aus den beiden konträren Körpern, spielen damit die beiden Schotten frei und lassen die gesamte Ausdehnung des Grundrisses erkennen. Im Obergeschoss können bis zu vier weitere Zimmer ausgebaut werden, entsprechend den Bedürfnissen der jungen Familie.

RESERVOIRSTRASSE DETACHED HOUSE, NEW CONSTRUCTION, BASEL
2014–2016

Two load-bearing walls, designed as bulkheads, define the long, staggered structure and frame it laterally. Following the course of the terrain, the first floor steps down to the garden, resulting in different room heights in the various living zones. An interior courtyard extends through the ground floor and basement, organising and illuminating the main living area as well as the master bedroom with dressing room and bathroom. The courtyard's counterpoint is the entrance area core containing a bathroom. All fixtures emerge from these two contrasting bodies, freeing the bulkheads and allowing the full extent of the floor plan to be perceived. Depending on the needs of the young family, up to four additional rooms can be constructed on the upper floor.

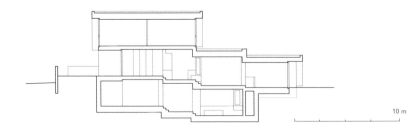

10 m

22

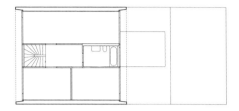

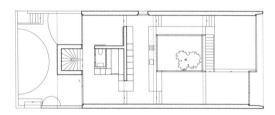

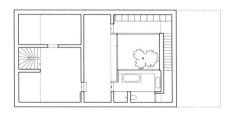

10 m

24

PUMPSTATION LANGE ERLEN, BASEL
2015–2020, Studienauftrag, 1. Preis

Das Pumpwerk Lange Erlen richtet sich dem Bestand folgend zur Hauptachse des Areals aus und schafft Platz für zukünftige Erweiterungen. Unter dem ausladenden Vordach der Eingangsfassade entwickelt sich ein aus Beton gefertigter Brunnen zunächst zur Sitzstufe und Treppe und dann weiter zur rollstuhlgängigen Rampe. Die Innenräume werden in Anlehnung an Gletschermühlen in sanften, ausgeschliffenen Rundungen ausformuliert. Aus diesen Rundungen wiederum entwickelt sich das grosse Oblicht im Foyer. Eine grosszügige Treppe windet sich um die Leuchte der Künstlerin Madlaina Lys zum eigentlichen Herzstück der Anlage: Von der Aussichtsplattform aus überblicken die Besucher die imposante Pumpenanlage.

LANGE ERLEN PUMPING STATION, BASEL
2015–2020, Contracted study, 1ˢᵗ Prize

Following the existing structure, the Lange Erlen pumping station is aligned to the main axis of the site and leaves space for future expansion. Under the projecting roof of the entrance façade, a concrete fountain transforms first into a bench and stairs and further along into a wheelchair-accessible ramp. The interior spaces are built with gentle, polished curves in emulation of glacial mills. These curves also give shape to the large skylight in the foyer. A generous staircase winds up around the light by the artist Madlaina Lys to the building's true centrepiece: the observation deck, from which visitors have a view over the extensive pumping facility.

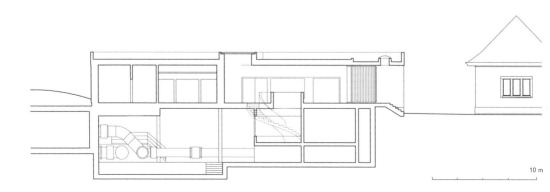

10 m

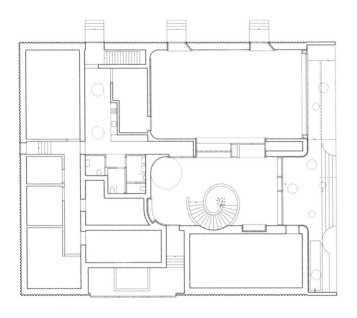

10 m

UMBAU EINFAMILIENHAUS PAPPELWEG, MUTTENZ
2017

Das 1969 von Burckhardt Architekten erbaute, durch Halbgeschosse geprägte Einfamilienhaus ist in seiner Struktur und Materialität seit der Bauzeit erhalten geblieben. Der überzeugende Bestand mit Decken aus Sichtbeton, Einbauten, Verkleidungen und Fenstern aus Holz sowie eine Fassade aus Sichtmauerwerk bildeten die Ausgangslage für den Umbau. Im Erdgeschoss wird die Raumschicht mit Entrée und Küche neu gegliedert. Die Küche vergrössert sich bis zur nordöstlichen Gebäudeecke, es werden Ess- und Wohnbereich in der Grundrissmitte zusammengeführt. Eine grosse Öffnung in der Wand, die die Galerie vom Dachstock trennt, schafft die kaskadenartige räumliche Verbindung aller Ebenen. Ein neu eingefügtes Treppenmöbel aus Beton, das sich zur Sitzbank und Ablage weiterentwickelt, erschliesst diese Ebenen.

PAPPELWEG DETACHED HOUSE CONVERSION, MUTTENZ
2017

The original structure and materiality of the detached house, built in 1969 by Burckhardt Architekten and characterised by mezzanine floors, has been preserved. With exposed concrete ceilings, wooden fixtures, coverings and windows, and a masonry façade, the existing building offered a compelling basis for conversion. On the ground floor, the room layer formed by the foyer and kitchen has been restructured. The kitchen extends to the house's north-eastern corner and the dining and living areas were brought together in the middle of the floor plan. A large opening in the wall separating the gallery from the attic creates a cascade-like spatial connection between all levels. Newly inserted concrete staircase furnishings, which develop into a bench and a storage area, open up these levels.

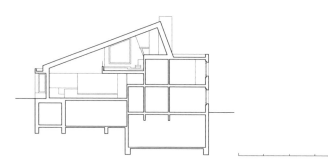

10 m

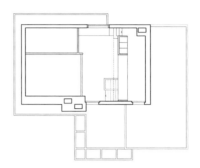

10 m

QUART

HIGHLIGHTS

2020/2

Peter Märkli – Everything one invents is true

Peter Märkli zählt seit den frühen 1980er-Jahren zweifellos zu den markantesten Deutschschweizer Architekten der ersten Stunde. Seine einprägsamen Bauten lassen sich jedoch nicht leicht in das Schema dieser Architekturbewegung einordnen. Zu sehr sind die einzelnen Bauwerke intensiv bearbeitete Individuen, die einer fortdauernden Bewegung des Suchens folgen. Immer eröffnen sie eigenständig und eindringlich Verbindungen der Geschichte der Architektur mit dem Impetus einer zeitüber-dauernden Gültigkeit.

Im vorliegenden Band sind 17 Bauten der letzten 15 Jahre mit Texten, Plänen und Abbildungen ausführlich dargestellt. Ergänzt wird die bemerkenswerte Werkdarstellung mit erhellenden Essays von Florian Beigel & Philip Christou, Franz Wanner und Ellis Woodman. Ein spannendes Interview mit Peter Märkli von Elena Markus und einzelne Statements des Architekten runden die eindrückliche Sammlung ab.

Herausgegeben von Pamela Johnston
Textbeiträge: Florian Beigel & Philip Christou, Pamela Johnston, Peter Märkli, Elena Markus, Franz Wanner, Ellis Woodman

240 Seiten, 29 × 29 cm
178 Abbildungen, 75 Pläne,
101 Zeichnungen
Hardcover, fadengeheftet
Englisch (teilweise übersetzt ins Deutsche *):
ISBN 978-3-03761-138-8
Englisch (teilweise übersetzt ins Japanische **):
ISBN 978-3-03761-139-5
CHF 138.– / EUR 126.–
* eingelegtes Booklet mit Essays in Deutsch
** eingelegtes Booklet mit Projektbeschrieben in Japanisch

Peter Märkli – Everything one invents is true

Since the early 1980s, Peter Märkli has been one of the most striking protagonists of German Swiss architecture from the earliest period of its emergence. However his impressive buildings cannot be easily classified in the scheme of this architectural movement, since the individual buildings are intensely developed individuals that follow the continuous movement of seeking. They always open up connections with the history of architecture in an independent, powerful way and express the impetus of timeless validity.

This volume presents 17 buildings in detail from the last 15 years with texts, plans and images. The remarkable presentation of works is complemented by enlightening essays by Florian Beigel & Philip Christou, Franz Wanner and Ellis Woodman. An exciting interview with Peter Märkli by Elena Markus and individual statements by the architects round off the impressive collection.

Edited by: Pamela Johnston
Articles by: Florian Beigel & Philip Christou, Pamela Johnston, Peter Märkli, Elena Markus, Franz Wanner, Ellis Woodman

240 pages, 29 × 29 cm
178 illustrations, 75 plans,
101 sketches
Hardback, thread-stitched
English (some texts also in German *):
ISBN 978-3-03761-138-8
English (some texts also in Japanese **):
ISBN 978-3-03761-139-5
CHF 138.00 / EUR 126.00
* with an enclosed booklet containing the essays in German
** with an enclosed booklet containing the project texts in Japanese

UMBAU MEHRFAMILIENHAUS FEIERABENDSTRASSE, BASEL
2017–2019

Das 1893 erbaute Wohnhaus nahe des Schützenmattparks wurde aufgrund des baufälligen Zustands grundlegend modernisiert und statisch verstärkt. Im Erdgeschoss entstand durch einen eingeschossigen Anbau eine grosszügige Familienwohnung. Um die Belichtung des tiefen Wohnungsgrundrisses zu gewährleisten, rückt der Anbau von der Gartenfassade ab und spannt einen kleinen Innenhof auf. Grossformatige Fenster machen den verwunschenen Garten bis tief in die Wohnung hinein spürbar. Aussen zeigt sich der Anbau in Sichtbeton, die Verkleidung im Inneren bilden rohe Birkensperrholzplatten. Durch das gartenseitige Anheben der Traufe entstand im Dachgeschoss ein ausladender Wohnraum mit durchgehender Fensterfront und vorgelagerter Terrasse.

FEIERABENDSTRASSE APARTMENT BUILDING CONVERSION, BASEL
2017–2019

In a dilapidated state, the residential house built in 1893 near Schützenmattpark was thoroughly modernised and structurally reinforced. On the first floor, a spacious family home was created by a new single-story extension. To illuminate the apartment's deep floor plan, the extension is detached from the garden façade to create a small interior courtyard. Large-format windows allow the enchanting garden to be perceived deep within the apartment. The exterior consists of fair-faced concrete, while the interior is finished with raw birch plywood panels. The raised eave on the garden side created an expansive living area with a continuous glass façade and a terrace towards the rear.

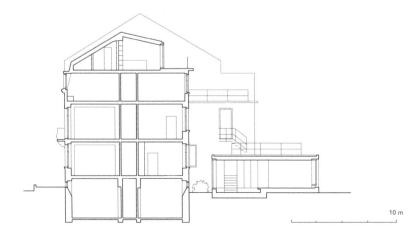

10 m

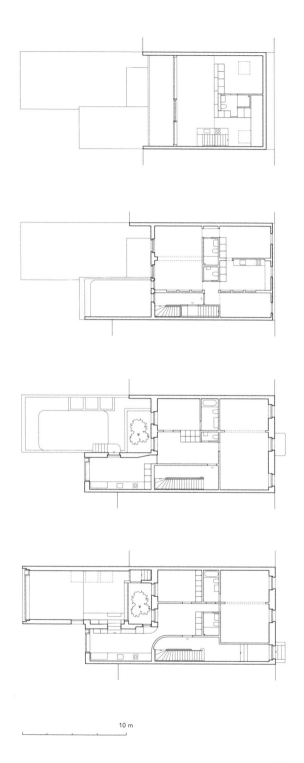

10 m

52

WERKVERZEICHNIS
Auswahl Bauten, Projekte und Wettbewerbe

2011		Umbau Reihenhaus Biascastrasse, Basel
	1	Dachstockausbau Scheune Isenbergstrasse, Ottenbach
		Umbau Wohnung Hauensteinstrasse, Basel
		Umbau Wohnung Im Sesselacker, Basel

2011   Umbau Reihenhaus Biascastrasse, Basel
  1   Dachstockausbau Scheune Isenbergstrasse, Ottenbach
       Umbau Wohnung Hauensteinstrasse, Basel
       Umbau Wohnung Im Sesselacker, Basel

2012 2 Umbau Mehrfamilienhaus Bartenheimerstrasse, Basel
         Wohnungsausbau Mönchaltdorferstrasse, Egg ZH
         Umbau Einfamilienhaus Wiesenstrasse, Oberwil,
         Mitarbeit: Raquel Gomez Sanchez

2013   Dachstockausbau Thumringerstrasse, Basel,
         Mitarbeit: Raquel Gomez Sanchez

2014 3 Doppeleinfamilienhaus Lättestrasse, Birmenstorf,
         Mitarbeit: Richard Robatel (Projektleitung)
         Umbau Einfamilienhaus Fasanenstrasse, Reinach,
         Mitarbeit: Michael Gunti
         Umbau Einfamilienhaus Biederthalstrasse, Rodersdorf,
         Mitarbeit: Raquel Gomez Sanchez
  4   Dachstockausbau und Sanierung Storchengasse, Brugg,
         Mitarbeit: Raquel Gomez Sanchez
         Doppeleinfamilienhäuser Rütiring, Riehen,
         Mitarbeit: Chiara Friedl (Projektleitung), Irina Zindel, Vitus
         Lachmann

2015   Studienauftrag Pumpstation Lange Erlen, Basel, 1. Preis,
         mit Fontana Landschaftsarchitektur, Basel,
         Mitarbeit: Nadine Strasser (Projektleitung), Kora Balmer,
         Valerian Wagner
  5   Umbau und Anbau Einfamilienhaus Marignanostrasse, Basel,
         Mitarbeit: Vitus Lachmann
  6   Umbau Einfamilienhaus Zehntenfreistrasse, Bottmingen,
         Mitarbeit: Sandra Villiger (Projektleitung)

2016 7 Einfamilienhaus Mayenfelserstrasse, Pratteln,
         Mitarbeit: Kora Balmer (Projektleitung), Sandra Villiger
         Einfamilienhaus Reservoirstrasse, Basel,
         Mitarbeit: Nadine Strasser (Projektleitung)
         Sanierung Mehrfamilienhaus Maulbeerstrasse, Basel
         Wettbewerb Pfarreigebäude, Ins, 2. Runde,
         Mitarbeit: Nadine Strasser, Kora Balmer

2017   Umbau Einfamilienhaus Pappelweg, Muttenz
         Umbau Einfamilienhaus Grünfeldstrasse, Allschwil,
         Mitarbeit: Valerian Wagner
         Umbau Einfamilienhaus Haltenstrasse, Obfelden
  8   Umbau Einfamilienhaus Chrischonaweg, Riehen,
         Mitarbeit: Simone Leuenberger (Projektleitung),
         Veronika Ferdinand
         Umbau Wohnung Höfliweg, Zürich,
         mit Nicholas Frei, Zürich
         Studie Baumhaus, Mitarbeit: Rodrigo Faria e Maia

1

2

3

4

LIST OF WORKS
Selection of buildings, projects and competitions

2011		Biascastrasse terraced house conversion, Basel
	1	Isenbergstrasse barn attic fit out, Ottenbach
		Hauensteinstrasse apartment conversion, Basel
		Im Sesselacker apartment conversion, Basel
2012	2	Bartenheimerstrasse apartment building conversion, Basel
		Mönchaltdorferstrasse apartment fit out, Egg ZH
		Wiesenstrasse detached house conversion, Oberwil, Collaboration: Raquel Gomez Sanchez

5   2013   Thumringerstrasse attic fit out, Basel,
Collaboration: Raquel Gomez Sanchez

2014	3	Lättestrasse semi-detached houses, Birmenstorf, Collaboration: Richard Robatel (Project Manager)
		Fasanenstrasse detached house conversion, Reinach, Collaboration: Michael Gunti
		Biederthalstrasse detached house conversion, Rodersdorf, Collaboration: Raquel Gomez Sanchez
	4	Storchengasse attic fit out and renewal, Brugg, Collaboration: Raquel Gomez Sanchez
		Semi-detached houses, Rütiring, Riehen, Collaboration: Chiara Friedl (Project Manager), Irina Zindel, Vitus Lachmann

6   2015   Lange Erlen Schorenweg pumping station contracted study, Basel, 1st prize, with Fontanta Landschaftsarchitektur, Basel, Collaboration: Nadine Strasser (Project Manager), Kora Balmer, Valerian Wagner

        5   Marignanostrasse detached house conversion and extension, Basel, collaboration: Vitus Lachmann

        6   Zehntenfreistrasse detached house conversion, Bottmingen, Collaboration: Sandra Villiger (Project Manager)

2016   7   Mayenfelserstrasse detached house, Pratteln, Collaboration: Kora Balmer (Project Manager), Sandra Villiger

Reservoirstrasse detached house, Basel, Collaboration: Nadine Strasser (Project Manager)

Maulbeerstrasse apartment building renovation, Basel

Rectory building competition, Ins, 2nd stage, Collaboration: Nadine Strasser, Kora Balmer

2017   Pappelweg detached house conversion, Muttenz

Grünfeldstrasse detached house conversion, Allschwil, Collaboration: Valerian Wagner

Haltenstrasse detached house conversion, Obfelden

8   Chrischonaweg detached house conversion, Riehen, Collaboration: Simone Leuenberger (Project Manager), Veronika Ferdinand

Höfliweg apartment conversion, Zurich, With Nicholas Frei, Zurich

Treehouse study, collaboration: Rodrigo Faria e Maia

8

2018	9	Einfamilienhaus Rütiring, Riehen,

2018   9   Einfamilienhaus Rütiring, Riehen,
Mitarbeit: Nadine Strasser (Projektleitung)
Einfamilienhaus Untere Leestrasse, Remingen,
Mitarbeit: Veronika Ferdinand, Alice Deprez

        10   Umbau und Erweiterung Einfamilienhaus Schäferstrasse, Riehen,
Mitarbeit: Rodrigo Faria e Maia, Mathias Schaub

        11   Umbau Reihenhaus Im Römergarten, Therwil,
Mitarbeit: Simone Leuenberger, Veronika Ferdinand
Studie Umnutzung Büroliegenschaft Clarastrasse, Basel,
Mitarbeit: Laura Traub, Matthias Keller, Alice Deprez
Umbau Einfamilienhaus Joachimsackerstrasse, Bottmingen,
Mitarbeit: Mathias Schaub (Projektleitung), Laura Traub
Wettbewerb Hallenbad Blumenwies, St. Gallen, 2. Runde,
Mitarbeit: Veronika Ferdinand, Rodrigo Faria e Maia, Laura Traub

9

2019   12   Umbau Mehrfamilienhaus Oetlingerstrasse, Basel,
Mitarbeit: Matthias Keller (Projektleitung), Laura Traub

        13   Umbau Mehrfamilienhaus Wielandplatz, Basel,
Mitarbeit: Nadine Strasser (Projektleitung), Alice Deprez

        14   Umbau Einfamilienhaus Rietstrasse, Ebmatingen,
Mitarbeit: Rodrigo Faria e Maia, Alice Deprez

        15   Umbau Einfamilienhaus Waltersgrabenweg, Riehen,
Mitarbeit: Laura Traub

        16   Umbau Einfamilienhaus Brosiweg, Dornach,
Mitarbeit: Rodrigo Faria e Maia
Umbau Mehrfamilienhaus Feierabendstrasse,
Basel, Mitarbeit: Rodrigo Faria e Maia, Alice Deprez
Studienauftrag «Wohnen und was noch», Hamburg, DE,
Mitarbeit: Stephanie Doll, Veronika Ferdinand, Mathias Schaub
Studie Wohnhäuser Pfeffingen, Mitarbeit: Matthias Sutter,
Rodrigo Faria e Maia

10

2020   Pumpstation Lange Erlen, Basel,
Mitarbeit: Veronika Ferdinand (Projektleitung), Kora Balmer,
Mathias Schaub, Alice Deprez, Nadine Strasser
Umbau Mehrfamilienhaus Rebgasse, Basel,
Mitarbeit: Mathias Schaub (Projektleitung)
Dachstockausbau Im Sesselacker, Basel,
Mitarbeit: Matthias Sutter (Projektleitung), Stephanie Doll

11

12

13

14

15

16

2018	9	Rütiring detached house, Riehen, collaboration: Nadine Strasser (Project Manager)
		Untere Leestrasse detached house, Remingen, Collaboration: Veronika Ferdinand, Alice Deprez
	10	Schäferstrasse detached house conversion and extension, Riehen, collaboration: Rodrigo Faria e Maia, Mathias Schaub
	11	Im Römergarten terraced house conversion, Therwil, Collaboration: Simone Leuenberger, Veronika Ferdinand
		Clarastrasse office building conversion study, Basel, collaboration: Laura Traub, Matthias Keller, Alice Deprez
		Joachimsackerstrasse detached house conversion, Bottmingen, Collaboration: Mathias Schaub (Project Manager), Laura Traub
		Blumenwies indoor swimming pool competition, St. Gallen, 2nd stage, collaboration: Veronika Ferdinand, Rodrigo Faria e Maia, Laura Traub
2019	12	Oetlingerstrasse apartment building conversion, Basel, Collaboration: Matthias Keller (Project Manager), Laura Traub
	13	Wielandplatz apartment building conversion, Basel, Collaboration: Nadine Strasser (Project Manager), Alice Deprez
	14	Rietstrasse detached house conversion, Ebmatingen, Collaboration: Rodrigo Faria e Maia, Alice Deprez
	15	Waltersgrabenweg detached house conversion, Riehen, Collaboration: Laura Traub
	16	Brosiweg detached house conversion, Dornach, Collaboration: Rodrigo Faria e Maia
		Feierabendstrasse apartment building conversion and extension, Basel, collaboration: Rodrigo Faria e Maia, Alice Deprez
		"Wohnen und was noch" contracted study, Hamburg, DE, Collaboration: Stephanie Doll, Veronika Ferdinand, Mathias Schaub
		Housing study, Pfeffingen, collaboration: Matthias Sutter, Rodrigo Faria e Maia
2020		Lange Erlen pumping station, Basel, Collaboration: Veronika Ferdinand (Project Manager), Kora Balmer, Mathias Schaub, Alice Deprez, Nadine Strasser
		Rebgasse apartment building conversion, Basel, Collaboration: Mathias Schaub (Project Manager)
		Im Sesselacker attic fit out, Basel, Collaboration: Matthias Sutter (Project Manager), Stephanie Doll

STEPHAN MEYER

1979	geboren in Basel
1986–1990	Primarschule Basel
1990–1999	Gymnasium Kirschgarten, Basel, Matura Typus B
2000–2006	Architekturstudium an der ETH Zürich
	Diplom bei Christian Kerez
2002	Praktikum bei Christ & Gantenbein, Basel
2006–2010	Projektleiter bei Architekt André Kaufmann, Basel
2010	Gründung des Büros Staehelin Meyer Architekten
	mit Jonas Staehelin

JONAS STAEHELIN

1979	geboren in Zürich
1985–1991	Primarschule Ottenbach
1991–1993	Sekundarschule Obfelden
1993–1999	Kantonsschule Limmattal, Urdorf, Matura Typus C
1999–2000	Flight Attendant Swissair
2000–2006	Architekturstudium an der ETH Zürich
	Diplom bei Christian Kerez
2002	Praktikum bei Jean-Pierre Dürig Architekten, Zürich
2005	Praktikum bei Christian Kerez Architekten, Zürich
2007–2010	Projektleiter bei Buchner Bründler Architekten, Basel
2010	Gründung des Büros Staehelin Meyer Architekten
	mit Stephan Meyer

MITARBEITENDE

Kora Balmer, Alice Deprez, Stephanie Doll, Rodrigo Faria e Maia, Veronika
Ferdinand, Nils Frey, Chiara Friedl, Raquel Gomez Sanchez, Michael Gunti,
Matthias Keller, Vitus Lachmann, Simone Leuenberger, Richard Robatel, Mathias
Schaub, Nadine Strasser, Matthias Sutter, Laura Traub, Sandra Villiger, Valerian
Wagner, Irina Zindel

PUBLIKATIONEN, AUSSTELLUNGEN, VORTRÄGE

2012	Umbau Einfamilienhaus Biascastrasse Basel. In: Umbauen und Renovieren, 1/2012, S. 98–102
2015	Vortrag «Vorgestellt. Junge Basler Architekten», S AM, Basel
2016	Publikation «Schweizweit» zur gleichnamigen Ausstellung, S AM, Basel, S. 284–285
2018	Umbau Einfamilienhaus Pappelweg Muttenz. In: Auszeichnung Guter Bauten BL/BS 2018, S. 22–23 Umbau Einfamilienhaus Pappelweg Muttenz. In: Sonntagszeitung, 11/2018, S. 50
2020	Umbau Mehrfamilienhaus Feierabendstrasse Basel. Finalist «Der Beste Umbau 2019». In: Umbauen und Renovieren 1/2020, S. 111 Umbau Einfamilienhaus Pappelweg Muttenz. Ausstellung «Modern Living», Museum Kleines Klingental, Basel Pumpstation Lange Erlen Basel. In: Schweizer Baudoku-mentation, 5/2020, S. 52–61 Pumpstation Lange Erlen Basel. In: Hochparterre 10/2020, S. 57

STEPHAN MEYER

1979	Born in Basel
1986–1990	Primary school, Basel
1990–1999	Kirschgarten Secondary School, Basel, Matura Typus B
2000–2006	Studied Architecture at the ETH Zurich
	Diploma project with Christian Kerez
2002	Internship at Christ & Gantenbein, Basel
2006–2010	Project Manager at Architekt André Kaufmann, Basel
2010	Founded Staehelin Meyer Architekten with Jonas Staehelin

JONAS STAEHELIN

1979	Born in Zurich
1985–1991	Primary school, Ottenbach
1991–1993	Secondary school, Obfelden
1993–1999	Limmattal Cantonal School, Urdorf, Matura Typus C
1999–2000	Flight Attendant at Swissair
2000–2006	Studied Architecture at the ETH Zurich
	Diploma project with Christian Kerez
2002	Internship at Jean-Pierre Dürig Architekten, Zurich
2005	Internship at Christian Kerez Architekten, Zurich
2007–2010	Project Manager at Buchner Bründler Architekten, Basel
2010	Founded Staehelin Meyer Architekten with Stephan Meyer

COLLABORATORS

Kora Balmer, Alice Deprez, Stephanie Doll, Rodrigo Faria e Maia, Veronika Ferdinand, Nils Frey, Chiara Friedl, Raquel Gomez Sanchez, Michael Gunti, Matthias Keller, Vitus Lachmann, Simone Leuenberger, Richard Robatel, Mathias Schaub, Nadine Strasser, Matthias Sutter, Laura Traub, Sandra Villiger, Valerian Wagner, Irina Zindel

PUBLICATIONS, EXHIBITIONS, LECTURES

2012	"Biascastrasse detached house conversion", Basel. In: *Umbauen und Renovieren*, 1/2012, p. 98–102
2015	Lecture "Vorgestellt. Junge Basler Architekten", S AM, Basel
2016	Exhibition and publication *Schweizweit*, S AM, Basel
2018	Pappelweg detached house conversion, Muttenz. In: *Auszeichnung Guter Bauten* BL/BS 2018, p. 22–23
	Pappelweg detached house conversion, Muttenz. In: *Sonntagszeitung*, 11/2018, p. 50
2020	Feierabendstrasse apartment building conversion Basel. Finalist "Der Beste Umbau 2019". In: *Umbauen und Renovieren* 1/2020, p. 111
	Pappelweg detached house conversion, Muttenz. Exhibition Modern Living, Museum Kleines Klingental, Basel
	Lange Erlen pumping station, Basel. In: *Schweizer Baudokumentation*, 5/2020, p. 52–61
	Lange Erlen pumping station, Basel. In: Hochparterre 10/2020, p. 57

Finanzielle und ideelle Unterstützung

Ein besonderer Dank gilt den Institutionen und Sponsorfirmen, deren finanzielle Unterstützungen wesentlich zum Erscheinen dieser Buchreihe beitragen. Ihr kulturelles Engagement ermöglicht ein fruchtbares und freundschaftliches Zusammenwirken von Baukultur und Bauwirtschaft.

Financial and conceptual support

Special thanks to the institutions and sponsoring companies whose financial support makes a key contribution to the production of this book series. Their cultural engagement encourages fruitful, friendly interaction between building culture and the building industry.

Schweizerische Eidgenossenschaft
Confédération suisse
Confederazione Svizzera
Confederaziun svizra

Eidgenössisches Departement des Innern EDI
Bundesamt für Kultur BAK

ERNST GÖHNER STIFTUNG

BMF ProConsulting AG, Basel

Cadosch & Niederer Elektro-Installationen GmbH, Basel

DESAX AG, Gommiswald

EGELER LUTZ AG

Egeler Lutz AG, Basel

F Design Landscape AG, Bubendorf

Felix & Co. AG, Gebenstorf

Franz Maurer GmbH, Zürich

Gebrüder Schibli Bodenbeläge AG, Basel

Gilberto G. Versari
Eingefärbte Decorböden & Terrazzo
6363 Fürigen

Gilberto Versari, Fürigen

Hürzeler Holzbau AG, Magden und Basel

Krüsi Küchen AG, Allschwil

Makiol Wiederkehr AG, Beinwil am See

Salvo Caserta AG, Basel

Schibler AG, Muttenz

W. Lauper AG, Ettingen

Felix & Co. AG, Gebenstorf

Schreinerei Weber AG, Seewen SO

Alltech Installationen AG, Muttenz
GlobalBroker AG, Basel
Jürg Merz Bauing. HTL, Glarus und Maisprach
Raiffeisenbank Allschwil-Schönenbuch, Allschwil
Steudler Press AG, Basel

Staehelin Meyer
44. Band der Reihe Anthologie
Herausgeber: Heinz Wirz, Luzern
Konzept: Heinz Wirz; Staehelin Meyer, Basel
Projektleitung: Quart Verlag, Antonia Chavez-Wirz
Textlektorat Deutsch: Kirsten Rachowiak, München, DE
Übersetzung Deutsch-Englisch: Nicholas Elliott, Berlin, DE
Textlektorat Englisch: Benjamin Liebelt, Berlin, DE
Fotos: Archiv Staehelin Meyer, Basel; ausser: Ruedi Walti, Basel
S. 34, 36
Redesign: BKVK, Basel – Beat Keusch, Angelina Köpplin-Stützle
Grafische Umsetzung: Quart Verlag
Lithos: Printeria, Luzern
Druck: DZA Druckerei zu Altenburg GmbH, Altenburg

Staehelin Meyer
Volume 44 of the series Anthologie
Edited by: Heinz Wirz, Lucerne
Concept: Heinz Wirz; Staehelin Meyer, Basel
Project management: Quart Verlag, Antonia Chavez-Wirz
German text editing: Kirsten Rachowiak, Munich, DE
Translation German-English: Nicholas Elliott, Berlin, DE
English text editing: Benjamin Liebelt, Berlin, DE
Photos: Archiv Staehelin Meyer, Basel; except: Ruedi Walti,
Basel p. 34, 36
Redesign: BKVK, Basel – Beat Keusch,
Angelina Köpplin-Stützle
Graphical layout: Quart Verlag
Lithos: Printeria, Lucerne
Printing: DZA Druckerei zu Altenburg GmbH, Altenburg

Quart Verlag GmbH
Denkmalstrasse 2, CH-6006 Luzern
books@quart.ch, www.quart.ch

* Inserted booklet with translation